Love Affair~

A VENETIAN JOURNAL

Books by Wright Morris

Love Affair~

A VENETIAN JOURNAL

Wright Morris

HARPER & ROW, PUBLISHERS

New York, Evanston, San Francisco, London

Production coordinated by Chanticleer Press, Inc., New York
Printed and bound by Amilcare Pizzi, S.p.A., Milan, Italy

FIRST EDITION 1972

STANDARD BOOK NUMBER: 06-013092-X

LIBRARY OF CONGRESS CATALOG CARD NUMBER: 72-79683

Designed by Patricia Dunbar

For my wife

Marcel Proust:
When I went to Venice I found that my dream
had become—incredibly but quite simply—my address!

letter to Madame Straus

THESE PHOTOGRAPHS illustrate nothing, they seek to demonstrate nothing, but hopefully they reveal the intent to salvage something of a love affair with a wondrous city.

Venice is sinking, but slower than most of us, and the sea will be less harsh than her likely survival, ringed by motorcades.

—W. M.

*A*CCUSTOMED TO the bizarre, our friend from California has come to see for himself if we are living in Venice. We assure him that we are. A lease has been signed to insure our exile. Already my wife has been lost and found. Bells are ringing. The light seems to vibrate with their clamor. Our friend impatiently waits for this unaccustomed racket to stop. Through the gate at the entrance he has left open we watch a barge drift past, we hear the lap of water, we note the cases of Campari, Punt e Mes, and Coca-Cola. The man at the tiller—he leans on it like a fence rail—wears a striped T-shirt, the smile of a happy pirate. To my wife he waves. She is popular with pirates from the way she goes up and down the city's bridges. He is there and gone. There are shouts like a street brawl as he greets his friends.

*T*HE MIND-BOGGLING gift of Venice is that it has escaped the tyranny of wheels. The motor launch coughs, the exhaust pollutes the air, but man *walks*—he does not run for his life. Only time will accustom us to a fact so profoundly bizarre. Of all unreal cities, this is the one that has its roots deepest in the imagination. Men dreamed it up, and now it is sinking into the ooze that will preserve it. Venice submerged may well prove to be stranger than Venice preserved. The gondolas in the Piazza are merely a reminder that this city was born of illusion, and that what man takes from the sea, the sea will repossess. As if it were sugar'd the smog-polluted air crumbles the stones, discolors the marble, and adds the final refinement to our taste for mutilations, our love for man-made ruins.

*T*HE HAPPY FEW in Venice have a window on a garden. We are among the happy few, but our happiness is clouded. Venetian cats pad in and out of the window at night, transporting kittens, live bait, and the heads of fish. At the foot of our bed, on which they land with a plop, they launder and dry clean the family pelts, check on gains and losses, practice cat witchery. Their motors hum like refrigerators. There is one with one eye: it winks and flares like the flame of a match. We are cat people, and they seem to know it. The word has spread. By the light of morning we examine saucers tongue-buffed to gleam like enamel. Cat tracks on the table, cat hairs on the chairs, cat smears on my papers, but no visible cats. They are night strollers. During the day they go about masked. A carpenter has come to put a screen at the window, but the idea is novel and will take much reflection. While it is under advisement our new friends pad in and out.

*H*ER NAME is Dora. She acquired us in an involved transaction concerned with the washing of two bed sheets. The sheets are large, the color and weight of sailcloth, deliberately constructed to outlast the sleeper. But they are not easily washed. To be used as sheets, rather than a shroud, they have to be ironed. The first takes water, which is not in short supply; the second takes electric current that is sold by the drip, like maple syrup. We persuaded a lady in the Campo Santa Margherita (we saw her, Vermeer-like, ironing at an open window) to wash and iron our two sheets for 950 lire. That's a dollar and fifty cents, and it took her a week. This led to a discussion with the baker's wife on the curious scarcity of laundries in Venice. She had not heard about laundries. Anything that gets dirty is washed by a maid. Pillows are fluffed, rugs are beaten, children are watched and scolded by a housemaid. If one had a house, what one had to have next was a maid. Dora Rizzoli, a Rossellini-type woman, long accustomed to making crucial decisions, proved to be willing to wash and iron our sheets, and thereby acquired us.

*W*HAT is there to say?

My friend Pietro admits to the difficulty, but being Venetian he is not speechless. He spreads his hands in the manner of a man invoking rain. It's the muscles of the eye (he tells me) rather than the leg that are exercised. It is all solid stone—yet it is all illusion. For this effect one waits for the evening performance, and the lights come on. Stand at any point, look about you anywhere, and the figure of man is the measure. He is diminished, but not overpowered. He is exalted, but not exaggerated. Man is the measure here as he was in Athens, another colony of shrewd merchants. The gaze is horizontal, rather than up; the pigeons both maintain and establish proportion. Let that man with his eyes on heaven calculate the risks. No amount of gawking exhausts this prospect, and no amount of exposure depletes the impression. Amplitude and control, spiritual in its effect, sensible and secular in its practice. Pietro is now speechless. I am speechless. But this does not surround us with silence. A babble of tongues, a clamor of bells, and the music of three orchestras are now free to compete for our attention with the whirr of the world's greatest air force, as it comes and goes, performing intricate manoeuvres flawlessly.

Now THAT we are hers Dora bangs on counters and buys American soap flakes with a new assurance. The coupon that comes in the box she keeps for herself. For the Signora Morris, she says, as she orders, and then stops on the Zattere for an espresso. I am pointed out, as I pass, as a writer of American movies. She likes movies. She is eager to see those starring my wife. It also pleases Fabrizzio, the waiter, to be serving such a writer and movie mogul. Here in the sun on the Zattere things are looking up. He wipes off the seat where he wants me to sit. He serves with my espresso a paper napkin. That is unheard of. He reminds me one only lives once.

I do not write for the movies, I am no mogul, but in Venice I am less sure of this than elsewhere, the trompe l'oeil speaking with more persuasion than the facts. With Fabrizzio and Dora I have in common the instinct for fiction, the craving for illusion, and what is a mogul if he is not a purveyor of high romance?

*L*UIGI BONO sells beads and scarves, earrings for pierced ears only, money clips, postcards and maps of Venice, along with plastic gondolas and gondoliers that make gaily sorrowful music. This morning his stand is in the Campo Morosini. Tomorrow it may be elsewhere. Coming upon him in a new place is to renew and celebrate our friendship. The postcards and maps he sells to me. The beads he strings about the neck of my wife.

"Bellissima!" he cries. The beads are purple. What a surprise to find that purple is her favorite color. How should he know that? Was she ever in Chicago? Luigi's first cousin, Marcello, lives there. Because it is my wife, and the color is purple, he throws in, gratis, a packet of postcard views of Venice by night. The Festa del Redentore! Fireworks! Like a night bombing!

Luigi's buoyant good humor, his radiant optimism, is that of a long accustomed desperation. "Enjoy life!" he cries. Together, for a moment, we all make merry. He has beads to sell, and my wife has bought them. He feels good. She feels good. I feel generous.

*W*E BUY our milk, eggs, and cream (the cream is spooned from a bottle, the color and consistency of taffy) from Signora Pizzi, in order to hear her tote up the sums. Her recitation combines the style and voice of a tobacco auctioneer, punctuated by the fierce scratch of her pencil on the sheet of paper she folds about the eggs. We are impressed. Her husband stands mute with admiration. He follows her sonorous delivery, but the craft of the matter escapes him. What a woman he has! Signora Pizzi's hands have the color of pewter from the pouch of coins she wears at her waist. Most of them are alloy, leaden colored, and give off the sound of tiddlywinks. If I give her one presumed to be silver, she drops it on the counter as if she meant to crack it. No offense intended. Just an honest woman trying to live with thieves. One out of three of Signora Pizzi's eggs is far gone with child, may run a temperature, and should not be boiled. These facts are learned the hard way, and the good honest Signora no longer insists that the eggs be brought back to her for a sniff. She trusts my wife, who puts up two fingers to indicate the eggs we now get free. A basket of eggs sits on the counter, with the new ones at the bottom, the old ones at the top, but even the chicken, Signora Pizzi has observed, can make a mistake.

*O*UT OF shame we have not admitted that our real concern is not cats, but scorpions. Invisible cats we are long used to; invisible scorpions we are not. Scorpions do make handsome ornaments on the walls —and the first we noticed we thought to be ornamental—but on the crushed marble floors they cannot be seen until they move. Too often, in our opinion, that may be too late. I have been down on my knees to separate marble from scorpion. It is their nature to come up with the flowers in the spring, and then crawl up the walls into the windows of the happy people with garden apartments. At the *farmacia,* where I explained our problem, I was sold a tin of American Band-Aids. A more practical approach is to sprinkle DDT on the sills of garden windows, the powder providing a sure-fire method to track them down in the morning. Tracked down, they can then be encouraged to crawl up the walls. Dora can't seem to grasp why I'm so fidgety about something so small. Her own concern is limited to the rats she has seen climbing the vines in our garden, a creature I have hurried to assure my wife is a Venetian squirrel.

$\mathcal{M}$Y WIFE has learned from Dora that dishonest housemaids make off with the silver, with the hand-painted china, with the towels, the napkins, and the nylon panties; they swap old sheets for new ones, old soap for Ivory; they take aspirin from the bottles and sharp blades from the razors, coins from pockets, food from the refrigerator, stamps from the mail, cigarettes from the packets, and frequent snorts from the bottles with the imported labels. Honest housemaids, like herself, take only what they are given, which makes, in her opinion, for better relations. Observing me idle she naturally inquired what it was I did.

My wife replied, "He writes."

"For the movies?" My wife said no. "Which movies?" she asked. As a writer of movies, some of the good ones, it would explain what it is my wife sees in me. Otherwise it is a torment and a mystery. Her own husband, Vittore, sails away on freighters for as long as five months. What a relief that is! The thought of him brings on squalls of laughter. The thought of me a troubled silence. What do I *do?* Even my electric typewriter seldom works. Men are something she knows, and her glance assures me she has long known the worst.

*I*NSIDE the Bar Teatro, where we eat when it rains, our usual waiter is Alessandro. He is tall and efficient: in his solemn nature there is not one dram of the operatic. He has worked "around," like many Italians, and spent all of one summer on the coast of England. There he met and married an English girl. They have now lived two summers and one winter in Venice, and his wife, Rosalie, does not like it. She is not a tourist, enchanted by canals: she is the wife of a Venetian waiter. It is hard to find a place to live in Venice, unless you are a cat. She has seen the Piazza. She has been to Torcello. And she misses the sound of London traffic.

Alessandro asks my advice about migrating to the new world. He likes the sound of British Columbia. Where would that be? He is no painter, he is no writer, but he has the Venetian gift of illusion. He sees a great future in British Columbia, wherever it is. Rosalie finds the Italian language confusing and talks only to the English she meets in the Piazza. Alessandro feels sure she'll like the new world better, somewhere inland, away from all water, where there are birds without cages and flowers in the earth instead of a pot.

A WELL-TO-DO Venetian lady with a housemaid who sings, beats rugs, and plays records lives directly above us. The maid has the Italian love for volume—music that is not loud is simply not music. We have learned that some music is better than other music for beating rugs. As I listen the dust filters down to sparkle in the light that slants through our shutters. The dust of ages? How many times has it been beaten to rise, briefly sparkle, and allowed to settle? Here in Venice—as nowhere else—it is not an inexhaustible commodity. Housemaids could not do without what is beaten or shaken at one window, and falls to enter another. Twice I have thrown wide the shutters to shout the word *"Silenzio!"* to no effect. It sounds like a name. Perhaps she feels I am calling my wife. I often pass this prima donna at the door, back from shopping, in the green uniform of a schoolgirl. But it is no schoolgirl's glance she gives me. Considering their non-liberated status, Venetian girls rate high in assurance. All sing *"Arrivederci Roma"* as if they have lived there. Besides records, they collect shoes and a smattering of English useful in the tourist season. It's a girl that fits you for shoes in Venice, and may explain why so many are sold, the upward glance of their eyes costing you nothing as you ask the price.

ONE DAY A WEEK Dora polishes the silver, which may be why we are reluctant to use it. We use what we found in the kitchen drawer, assorted implements abandoned by the previous tenant. Forks with bent prongs outnumber the spoons; a can opener is neither in the drawer nor the dictionary. Another day a week Dora dusts around, airs the bedding at the window, mops the floor with an eye-burning disinfectant. All days of the week she greets my wife by lifting her from the floor, then twirling slowly until both are dizzy. About me she is less enthusiastic. *Buon giorno,* she says, but not like she means it. Dora's instincts are possessive, and we have been advised to count the silver each time she cleans it. How well she knows that! It brings a special zest to her work. Each piece of silver is down in the inventory, which runs to nineteen single-spaced typed pages. The screen at the windows has been added, but not the cats. More than four hundred books are in the house somewhere, along with many large paintings in the abstract manner, the landlord being an artist who hopes to live in Paris as long as we pay the rent.

*T*HE CAMPO SAN LUCA, with one exception, is as empty as mid-Sunday morning. The shops are shuttered, the streets and alleys are vacant except for a few souvenir-hungry tourists. A holiday, perhaps? Not one of those we find on the calendar. Custom decrees that every day is a holiday after lunch. These greedy merchants, although eager for the tourist dollar, close up shop right when the tourist wants to spend it—after eating, and fortified by, a good lunch. Simply because there is no time or place for the tourist to spend them, millions of lire are carried off elsewhere. But custom is custom.

I forget just when it was—it came so easy and naturally—we first kicked off our shoes and took a little nap. You've had the soup and the pasta, the cheese and the wine, the fruit and the espresso, and then you have the siesta. It was my wife who pointed out how accustomed to the custom we had become.

ON A MATTER of business we sit in the chambers of a young lawyer, his office in a *palazzo* on the Grand Canal. Out the towering window the *vaporetto* whistles. Framed in the window is a view painted by Canaletto. It is hard to keep in mind that we are here to protest a request that we pay taxes.

On what? On the furniture and property of the landlord. It has proved harder to collect from him than it might be from us. The lawyer makes doodles of a space-age nature as he calls City Hall. He speaks to the tax man. They exchange compliments like forehand volleys. Now he leans forward, his brow clouded, and he speaks for me, his client. All my life I have heard of sotto voce, and here, at last, I was hearing it spoken. By his smile I see that justice has triumphed, and—for the time being—we pay no taxes.

Before we depart he shows my wife the view down the canal to San Giorgio Maggiore, the water black as ink, the trees in the public gardens as fiercely green as an oasis. "What will his fee be?" my wife asks me, as we leave. I will find his bill under the door in the morning. From the Accademia bridge, where a breeze is rising, and Tiepolo's sky is glowing behind us, we are both thinking—we are all three thinking—that Venice is not something one should get for nothing, and such views should be taxed.

*I*T'S IMPORTANT to remember—I sit lecturing my wife—that many tourists in Venice are Italians. They honeymoon here. They bring their children. They stroll about and gawk like the folks from Des Moines. Two tables away—his knees spread to avoid collecting bread crumbs—a father lectures his son on Italian history. All around his soup plate crusts are strewn, like wood chips. His feeling for his subject makes him animated. He is a handsome man, of the Mastroianni type, with a wandering eye. That my wife is attentive enhances his performance. His son is like him. The boy wears shorts that display his plump Italian knees. It is a help that his wife is away, buying beads, while he impresses his son with history. The boy is not bored. He drinks his Coca-Cola through a straw and takes pride in his father's pride, his animation. That too sums up Italian life, and I appreciate the view of it they give me. Family ties. Italy a collection of Gordian knots. Venice is sinking, Florence is dying, Rome is rotting, the lira is falling, but what is Italian is not yet threatened. The father talks to his son. The son listens and watches his father eat soup.

*T*HE LITTLE WAITER, Paolo, goes out of his way to set up the table for the two ample hausfraus. They settle down like hens, clucking in German. He says, *"Oui, oui!* mademoiselles!" and has them laughing. They occupy a table for five people, but never mind. It matters little to Paolo what barbarians come to Venice to be charmed. Black and brown ones, thin and fat ones, good ones, bad ones, enemies and allies, bores and beauties, the merchants, pedlars and waiters of Venice will greet them with unexampled impartiality. One is reminded that Hitler loved Venice, and may have experienced a similar welcome. The Venetian is free of the dilemma of taking sides. He is pleased to see anybody come, and so that they may come again, he waits for them to go. His perspective comprehends a dismaying archive of history. Through the open-air lobby of the Piazza the great and the small have pursued their phantoms, somehow leaving in Venice more than they managed to take away. Barbarians come, barbarians go, dying Venice lives on.

CROM THE DECK of a *vaporetto,* or at the end of an alley where tilted poles mark a gondola mooring, the stranger in Venice may often feel that he sees, approaching over the water, the souls of the dead. The funereal barque glides toward him, or drifts silently by him, the occupants all standing, solemnly facing forward, as if making their final crossing of the River Styx. No head is turned, no word is spoken, until they clamor to the pier at the end of the crossing. A symbolic journey? They disperse rapidly without glancing back.

Although identified with carnival revelry, and dreams of romance, the gondola casts a black ominous shadow on the water. Gleaming black, the brass hardware polished, the *ferro* at the prow like an heraldic device, even the tasseled cords and opulent velvet cushions put the observer in mind of a watery hearse. Black. Why must the gondola be black? It is less a color than a state of soul, it appeals and gratifies below the level of discussion. Limousines are black, hearses are black, and black is the color of authority, mystery, and death. Powdered with snow the gondola is surreal, an object Marco Polo brought back from China, but any day of drizzle renews and enhances its appropriate aura of eternal mourning.

*A*T NIGHT the play of shadow, from low-wattage bulbs, adds drama to the ornate ceilings of Venice. We see them from the alley or *fondamenta* below, a passing glimpse through the half-shuttered window, suggestive of a life, of an opulence at odds with the decaying exterior. It has seldom been our luck, or our privilege, to see into these rooms from another perspective. We are ceiling voyeurs, alert to any suggestion of the life and times of the occupants. More often than not they sing or play records. Italians do not need showers to be inspired to song.

The coming of TV may well alter Venice more than the rising tides. The proud owner hurries home to watch it while eating, sharing the sound, if not the pictures, with his neighbors. The volume is high. Viewer response is often enthusiastic. In the winter this racket is muted by closed shutters, but on warm summer nights, the windows open, the flicker of the tube is like that of flashing bulbs or heat lightning. Our first season in Venice the TV was a glory visible on weekends in bars and cafés, where local citizens, seated on chairs, appeared to be watching a puppet show that came with the box. A mini-world of midgets with the voices of giants.

NUMBERLESS painters and writers have sunned and worked here
—a plaque nearby bears the name of John Ruskin—and shortly after
the war a few American painters discovered a Venice that had never
been lost. Today rusting freighters, moored on Giudecca, ride so high
out of the water they conceal the island, obscuring the view but pre-
serving the Zattere from the horde of resort tourists. There are no
beaches; there are no clubs; the nights are free of *le jazz* cool or hot.
Under the gay umbrellas there are more knitting matrons than dozing
painters or footsore tourists. White cruisers pass here, bound for Con-
stantinople. Occasionally a great steamer, to and fro New York, appears
to be docked in Lilliput, darkening the city like a cloud's shadow.
River tubs once seen along the Thames bear the *Herrenvolk* to Cyprus,
Greece, Mykonos. To leave Venice by steamer (unless it's in November,
and drizzling at the porthole) is to question your actions. Better to go
by land where the sense of loss is accurately described as returning
to earth.

My wife says, "Think of it! We've been here for four months." It
seems longer than that. It seems shorter than that. We think of it.

$\mathcal{E}$MILIO CASTELLO stands before me, holding up the stubby fingers of both hands. Eight bend down, reluctantly, as he counts aloud from *uno* to *otto*. On *otto* he cried, *"Ottanta! Ottanta!"* Perhaps he finds it harder to believe than I do. Eighty years is old for a beggar. He accepts, with thanks, the coins I give him. There are few beggars in Venice, and here in Dorsoduro, away from the tourists, coins are given without the moisture of pity. *"Vecchio! Vecchio!"* he shouts to me, in case I seem to doubt it. He doesn't know about Americans. Perhaps eighty to them is young. That he is *ottanta,* and *vecchio,* both amazes and humiliates him. Life is a burden, but not yet one that he is willing to put down.

*E*MILIO does not sing, dance, or do card tricks, leaving these crafts to his colleague, Giuseppe. That is sensible and shrewd, because Giuseppe has no equal. There are some who say he has no talent. He is small, hung with offsize clothes, the pockets of his coat bulging with newspapers. His manner is that of a reluctant bailiff. One looks up to see him, in a crowd of empty tables, looking for precisely the *right* table. How can he choose? He waves off a clutter of invisible pigeons. Now that he has our attention (he has never lacked it) he takes from a pocket (one on the inside) the loose pages of a book, which he shuffles like cards. He fans them out to consider their message, selects two, returns the rest to his pocket. These two pages he holds before him, and waits patiently for silence. A boat drifts by. A *vaporetto* is allowed to arrive and depart. Now he sings. One is so sure that he sings the silence is disconcerting. We strain to listen. No one in Venice gets such total attention. His gaze is upward. His mouth shapes words that emerge from his lips like bubbles, visible but unheard. When he is finished he bows, then raises one hand to interrupt the applause. From his head he takes the hat that he passes among us, giving it a shake to estimate the coins, a man who knows his work.

IN GIUSEPPE'S melancholy performance there is something older than Venice. A perfectionist, his expression is anxious. He seats himself at a table to count the coins, exchanging them for paper money with Fabrizzio, the waiter. Fabrizzio is not at ease with a man of such unusual talents. What is one to make of him? Is he merely crazy? He is also a Jew, and that might explain it. An Italian would sing, once he had opened his mouth. It is thought inappropriate to laugh at Giuseppe, since it might reflect on his intentions. But not to laugh takes training. My eyes film over. A lump swells in my throat. I have seen him at a table in the Piazza reading the London *Daily Mail* and sipping cognac, now and then lifting his eyes to glance wearily at the spectacle. I have also seen him at the Punta della Salute dangling a fishline in the water, a half-dozen or so cats gathered around him to eat his catch.

$\mathcal{N}$EAR SAN GIORGIO DEGLI SCHIAVONI, made holy by Carpaccio, the alley we followed ended in a court where a piece of bent pipe provided a fountain. A big white and grey tomcat, indifferent to our intrusion, stood erect as if to snatch fish from the stream of water, his left paw delicately placed on the bent pipe for balance. In that posture he took little bites of the water, as the dogs of my boyhood took it from sprinklers, or garden hoses. Between bites, showing his long pink tongue, he licked the drops from his cheeks and whiskers. His thirst sated, still indifferent to us, he took himself off.

"What a picture!" cried my wife, "did you get it?"

I got one, but not the other. I had settled for the blurred, vulnerable impression on my mind's eye. More basic than my impulse to capture the moment had been my instinct not to disturb it. My eyes were not so sharp as the lens of the camera but they would prove to have a wider field of vision. The cat that got away, of all the cats in Venice, would prove to be the most memorable. The camera confronts the traveller with a choice of impressions—a souvenir that is sharp, and goes into his album, or one that is unrecorded, fragmentary, doomed to fade, and inexhaustible.

*C*OME STA?" he shouts.

I reply *"Va bene!"* I have found him again, my friend Luigi. Here he is in the Campo Santa Margherita, strong with the smell of fish this morning. Dumbfounded he asks how in such a short time I speak such stupendous Italian. His excitement—and my Italian—attracts customers, prospective buyers. He cranks up the plastic gondola that plays *"O Sole Mio,"* as the gondolier paddles. Sensing a handout, pigeons materialize, strut at our feet. We have a small-scale *festa* going until a blue-rinsed poodle, dragging his leash, scatters the birds and eludes all pursuers. The confusion is Venetian: Luigi bellows, my wife shrieks, and a squadron of pigeons, like low-flying jets, darken the Campo with their pale, wavering shadows, the air sparkling with debris that falls, just like old times, into our upturned eyes. Luigi and I wait calmly while my wife gropes in her purse for her mirror.

*T*HAT DORA and my wife do not speak a common language has cemented their relationship. I hear their shrieks of laughter. The occasion is a hat brought over from the new world, placed on the old world head of Dora. It does something for her. My wife can find something Venetian for herself. That is true of my raincoat—how well it fits Dora! —and hadn't I been planning all this time on a new one? My weakness for Italian shoes is approved by Dora—my old ones fit one of her many relations. It is liberating, this new feeling, to be a contributing member of such a large family. I see one of my ties on a waiter in the Piazza. I had thought his keen interest in me was impartial.

Now that Dora has us—now that she has so much to lose—she would prefer that we sleep with closed and latched shutters. The empty garden now teems (she is sure) with thieves who squeeze through bars and climb like scorpions. Why otherwise are the tops of garden walls planted with broken glass and the fragments of bottles? A chilling sight. In all our long days we have not been robbed, but we are now native Venetians in our apprehension. If we go to the Piazza, or out for an espresso, we must latch up tight or accept the consequences: no electric typewriter to run hot, when it works, no portable record player that gives off shocks when I plug it in.

*T*HERE IS more than a touch of the Mardi Gras in the Festa del Redentore. The tourist is overwhelmed. The entire population of Venice can be seen in migration, crowding the narrow alleys, crossing pontoon bridges put up by the army, a lemming-like exodus to the island of Giudecca where the holiday is climaxed by fireworks. Venetians with boats float darkly on the water, occasionally lit up by the flares of rockets, revealing mama, a child in her arms, tilting the prow toward heaven as she gives the skiff ballast. The rest jam the promenades or occupy, for hours, the chairs and tables of the sidewalk cafés. They do not eat, talk, drink or make merry: they sit silently and wait for the fireworks.

For Fabrizzio, this spectacle dissolves his love and compassion for his fellowmen. After *one* espresso, *one* glass of cheap wine, *one* Punt e Mes, or *one* Coca-Cola, a Venetian is entitled to sit as long as he likes, and this night he sits long. Those who do not sit—packs of moiling, loutish youths—hoarsely bark at each other and whistle at females. Fireworks prepare the sky for miracles. Long after midnight, safe in bed, we hear shouts like barbarians sacking Rome. As visitors from a country where such play is in earnest, we are glad the gate is locked, the windows barred. These celebrants, however, a few flushed with wine, the majority glutted with pizzas and Coca-Cola, trek their raucous way through the alleys of Venice and go quietly to bed.

A SUMMER Sunday in Venice, throbbing with bells, dazzling with heat and light or prostrate under the sirocco, gathers under one sky all the Sundays of the world that never seem to end. In the cooling dusk the eyes and the spirit may recover briefly, to gaze upward at a sky like emeralds, but there is still the shuttered night to be lasted, the howling and strumming from the tourist barges, some of them trailing gondolas like coffins, adding the appropriate Venetian refinement to Dante's hell. Blending with the soaring arias from the barges, their strings of carnival lights shimmering on the water, strains of "Home on the Range," or "Moonlight on the Wabash," sung with the strident passion of the homesick exile, provide the ultimate lament for souls resigned to a watery grave.

*I*T IS my impression that the women of Venice provide the cement that holds the stones together. Cries that Venice is sinking, or crumbling, are the cries of men. Men can be seen here and there in Venice doing more than selling beads or taking money from tourists, but the coffee is ground, the olive oil is poured, the pasta is measured, the potatoes are weighed, the sheets are washed, and the flowers watered by women. One of the women we know, a vegetable merchant, has a man who sets her stand up in the morning, then he goes off to fish until it is time to take it down. He is a good setter-upper, he makes good babies, he lifts heavy boxes, and he is no trouble. Side on he looks like Botticelli, but front on his gaze wanders. You should see him as he leans on the wall, peeling an orange, or reclines in his boat reading the cartoon classics. He, too, has heard talk (circulated by tourists) that the stones are crumbling, that Venice is sinking—one of many rumors that he sensibly refers to his wife.

*T*HE UNSIGNED MURALS of Venice, hung in plein air, compete favorably with those displayed at the Biennale. They are old in subject but modern in taste, avant-garde in their harmony of color and texture. The instinct for the ready-made and labelled object comprehends the ready-made and framed abstraction. Walls, doorways and windows, patterns of bricks and mortar, peeling strips of plaster with the gloss of leather, colors blended by time and mixed by the weather, graffiti and collages, the assembly of devices, emblems, and symbols in the gondola seem to be lacking nothing but the signature of the artist. If everyone is an artist—a currently fashionable notion—Venice provides everyone with his own ready-made work of art.

*T*HE BUTCHER'S SON, a lad not yet in his teens, wraps the package for his father and closes the door to the freezer. His excitement to grow up and be his own butcher shines in his eyes. The tobacconist's boy, who might be going on seven, sells us stamps and makes change as he practices his English. His father observes him. He gives us to know he did the same thing himself, only younger. The boy is all ears when his father talks, all eyes when he observes how stamps are torn, in strips, to simplify the calculation. He is also all boy, his learning complicated by the hard candy melting in his mouth, the admiring attention he gets from my wife. "O-keh?" he says, putting the coins on the counter. His father cautions him not to be so forward. His business has grown—souvenirs clutter the counter, and the tobaccos of the world crowd his small accommodations—but he is not such a fool as to spoil it all by hiring help. "Chesterfeels, Elun-M, Gamuls!" chants the boy. His father knows that my wife smokes Nazionales. A smart woman. If it all goes up in smoke, at least it should be cheap. Father and son exchange glances: next time he will know better. His mother comes from the back to assure my wife that the son is just like his father, excellent with figures, subject to summer colds he cannot shake off.

VENETIAN dogs are muzzled, but opinion varies as to which end of the dog should wear it. The limbs of both natives and tourists are threatened by the droppings in the narrow alleys. The dogs' feelings have not been aired, but they can be guessed. Except for a few gardens, fenced off like convents, they live in a stone-floored dungeon of canals and bridges. How long will it take to breed the scratch out of a Venetian dog? Numberless generations of Venetian cats show no modifications in their cat-like habits. They breed, scavenge, doze and howl in their traditional feline manner. I've watched a local tabby, an accomplished tumbler, adjust the urgent demands of nature to a four-inch pot of prickly cactus, manoeuvring, with elegance and patience, to accept life on the terms given. Not all cats in Venice, however, have it so difficult. In the shop where we buy our olive oil and coffee there is a box of fresh dirt for the Master's convenience, and the big cat snoozes on the seat of the chair while the elderly Signora leans on the counter to rest her feet. The bell he wears is ornamental; his taste runs to clam sauce, tinned tuna, and fresh popsicle sticks.

*T*HESE October days we've had barges from Chioggia, painted like banners, moored in the Rio di San Trovaso. The men sleep on the decks. We see them plainly at the end of the tunnel that leads to our garden. Lanterns gleam in the hold where they sit eating: they glance at me with the eyes of men sorting booty. These sea dogs are another race from Venetians, they have the air of whalers among city people. Their voices have a deeper register: it pleases me that their speech smacks of far away places. I think of wandering Greeks, of affluent Phoenicians, of barbarians who raid and loot by water. As the sky cools, the light of dusk enhances the color of their barges. The city before them lies waiting to be ravished, while the leaders discuss the terms of the ransom. The mood is optimistic. A carnival will celebrate the settlement. In the morning, however, I am pleased to find them gone, having sailed at dawn for Byzantium, their holds crowded, their decks jammed with impressions that remain unchallenged. We did not come here to gawk at sea dogs who had lost their bite.

*B*EFORE WE KNOW where we are, we sense that it is different. I feel obliged to estimate how many people once lived, or still live, in this mass-housing experiment. It is spare of ornament (except for the laundry) and obviously holds to the rules of tenement housing. Nowhere else in Venice is there a wall of windows calculated to suggest a human hive. One thinks of numbers. The numbers game had its beginning here in Venice, and this is one of the first solutions. A ghetto. A place set aside for fleeing Jews.

The ghetto may well be a Venetian invention (until some other city claims it) but the word is too charged with history not to feel its awesome presence. The persistence of the ghetto is recorded in the words *vecchio, nuovo, novissimo*—old, new, and newest—but there is little in the atmosphere today to suggest it will go on forever. The wall of windows, like a reflection on water, appears to undulate as in an earth tremor, the flags and banners of the corporate laundry hang limp as the ship goes under. In a city of grand illusions, this illusion is unforgettable.

*D*ORA WEARS all of her jewels, and advises my wife to do the same. One's person, one's life, is safe in Venice, but anything portable is up for grabs. The Venetian thief is a cat-footed chap who follows the rules like a good soccer player—only he's not so well paid. My own feeling is he'd do much better elsewhere, but Venetians are notorious homebodies. What's to be found in a snatched purse that will cost him the light in the Piazza?

One night I left my keys in another pair of pants and there we were, about midnight, locked and shuttered out. The man who owns the local bar, an ex–soccer player, showed us how a clever thief would enter our locked-up house. He scaled the wall like Douglas Fairbanks, and opened the shutters to the bathroom with a beer can opener. Everything went according to Hoyle until he got inside and fell on the stairs. As he assured me later, it's the inside of the house that scares a good thief.

—AND THEN there are days, often a run of days, hot and humid, or chill and indifferent, when the customary veils drop from our eyes and we see it, feel it, and smell it for what it is, a vast dungeon moated by fetid water, where spirits circulate with the pallor of corpses, their bony heels clacking in the narrow alleys, the fuming vapors of hell rising from canals that have been drained (it is rumored) to be cleaned and repaired, and the crowd flowing over the Bridge of Sighs is on its doomed way to where all must follow—

       so many,

       I had not thought death had undone so many

but these days pass, the vapors vanish, the symptoms of malaise and disorder prove phantoms, and no illusion is harder to recover than the one that seemed the least illusive, the most obvious.

*W*ITHIN THE larger maze—the two halves of the city that clutch each other, like the heads of serpents—there are islands, or separate countries with their own bridges and moats. Our own quarter combines the flavor of a seaport and left bank. The wide promenade is lined with sidewalk cafés, the water shimmering with the reflections of marble façades and striped umbrellas. The tables are on platforms, floating on the sea, and with the arrival and departure of a *vaporetto* the water slaps underfoot and the platform rocks like the deck of a ship.

As a rule we dine à la carte, because we are smart and know how to save money. Minestrone is nothing; spaghetti con burro is nothing; the green salad is nothing; the wine is nothing; the espresso and brandy to follow are nothing. The secret of success in the café business is the à la carte menu of numberless nothings. We have been living here, months now, on almost nothing—until we add it up.

*D*ISTANCE in Venice is a matter of taste, the time one prefers between stops for an espresso. One will get me from the house to the Piazza, but three will be required to get me back. The city is designed to meet this need and one is seldom far from the smell of strong coffee, the hiss of steam that gives strength to the weary. The machine itself defies accounting, a marvel of valves, levers, and grace under pressure, cunningly designed to emphasize how much it takes to make so little. Into this fragrant essence the initiate dissolves an almost equal amount of sugar, then sips it in the manner of a liqueur or tosses it off like a shot of whiskey. The spoon is used to salvage the puddle of sugar at the bottom of the cup.

Today Antonio, our waiter, writes on his pad what he is in the mood to serve us. This evening it will be pizzas. They come hot from the furnace, simmering and fragrant. On the cooling sky the streaks and cries of swallows. Passing tourists draw close to our table to see what we are eating. A three-pawed cat, his fourth limb a crutch, shoulders his way through cooing lovesick pigeons to our table, a true Venetian example of making do with whatever you've got.

A FRIEND from the States, his lips pursed but smiling, has been visiting with us for three ill-at-ease days. He is one for whom the bells of Venice toll a ceaseless, conspicuous message. No need for him to ask for whom the bell tolls—that is obvious. As we sit here talking the tide is rising, the water laps the boards underfoot. He arrived with a copy of *Death in Venice,* but he lacks the appetite to read or discuss it. If we take the *vaporetto* to Murano or Torcello it is for him a symbolic journey. The problem is the water: in the sun it dances, in the shade its depths chill the soul. Of all the cities he might have chosen, Aschenbach was right in choosing Venice. In a ceremony that requires no elaboration, as transparent to the stranger as the native, the Venetian makes his last watery crossing to the cypress island of San Michele, seamlessly intermingling the real and the illusory, the quick and the dead.

I'VE BEEN TELLING my friend Pietro that Henry James sat here, regally sipping tea. Pietro is impressed. Little he cares about Henry James, but he respects the past. After all, what else is there? In Venice one sees the present in the orderly perspective of history. No one ever suspects it of being all there is. The paintings of Bellini, in the Accademia, are like windows that open out on a city where little has changed. Carpaccio walked here, observing the costumes; Veronese and Titian observing the women. Aschenbach passed here on his way to the Lido, pausing to have his face repainted. To wear a mask, to play a role, is to do no more than what comes naturally. From the crowded wings one steps with assurance to the center of the stage. At the edge of the footlights, their decks crowded, boats shuttle between enchanted islands, yet in this city of water, from where I stand in the Piazzetta, no water is visible. It is the props that are moving, as if the city itself was being towed out to sea.

In an abandoned eastern quarter, crossing a bleak *campo,* we made our way through and among a troupe of actors in the midst of an historical movie. Swords clashed. Suits of armor clattered as soldiers bearing spears pursued a young man and a maiden in the guise of a priest. Through his megaphone the distracted director asked us to please move a little faster. Who did we think we were? I thought it a good question. In Venice we are all actors seeking new options, in search of new roles. When I thought about it later I felt that his movie would have been better if we had been in it. A prophetic touch! Tourists fleeing the pressures of history. A little confusing, perhaps, but truer to Venice, where the dejà vu is truer to life. The time machine in Venice runs forward and backward, and the instant replay is one of its innovations. One moment you are on the lip of the future, then careened into the past. If there is a questionable illusion in Venice it is what one assumes to be real in the present, like the daily news.

*T*HERE ARE natives of Venice, it is solemnly sworn, who have never set eyes on the Piazza San Marco, or the terra firma of Italy proper, a corner of Venice being more than enough to satisfy the need for travel. Hundreds of thousands of tourists now wander through Venice lifting their eyes from maps to search for signs, and then go off in the wrong direction. Those who reach the Piazza, unaided, are sometimes persuaded to settle for it. Have they not seen Venice? Is there any reason for pushing their luck? The labyrinthine maze of streets and alleys, frequently ending at the edge of the water, reinforce the impression (common to weary travellers) that they have come here to get lost. No city has so many endings and so few beginnings visible on the maps.

*W*E ARE at home in Venice. We have a lawyer to defend us, a consul to befriend us. We have a *come sta* acquaintanceship with dozens of pedlars, waiters, shopkeepers and beggars, but after seven months in Venice what we know best are the ceilings of rooms we see through half-closed shutters. We are not among the have-nots, and locked out, but we are not asked in. Our neighbor, the handsome and gallant art scholar, who collects art objects it takes strong men to deliver, kisses the hand of my wife when we meet and asks me about the state of the American novel. His wife has told him that she has laughed very hard at one of my books, translated into Italian. Is that my intention? Or is it, as so often, the translation? He seems eager to discuss the question. He regrets hearing that we plan to leave.

We have been welcome, impartially treated, and now our departure is cordially awaited. That is one of the rules, not a deprivation, since the best Venetian social life is in public. Home is where one eats, shouts, takes siesta, and watches TV.

*W*E HAVE BEEN packing for days, but at the sight of our luggage —much more than we arrived with—Dora's grief is boundless. Her recovery is quick, however, to make certain we leave nothing to the landlord. Her booty accumulates. Already she makes plans for us to come again. There is a villa on the Rio San Vio, with a gondola mooring at the gate to the garden. Her eyes shine! What a place for the wife of a writer of movies! Once more she lifts my wife, they twirl dizzily, and she departs with what we can't take with us. A first installment. Her son will come with his boat for what remains.

From the deck of the steamer it is easy to believe that the sea is rising, and Venice is sinking. A high tide laps the Zattere promenade where Dora stands in the drizzle, crying *"Arrivederci!"* Her plans call for our return in April. In the comfort of the bar a boy from Giudecca (how can I be sure he is not one of Dora's?) reassures my wife, as he shakes our martinis, that if we are to come again to Venice, first we must depart.